D0124875

WHAT WOMEN SAY ABOUT MEN

Ariel Books

Andrews and McMeel

Kansas City

Witty Observations on the Male of the Species

What
Women
Say
About
Men

ISBN: 0-8362-3030-2

Library of Congress Catalog Card Number:
92—73436

INTRODUCTION

I n the Bible we find out everything there is to know about Adam's feelings. We know what *he* thinks about the expulsion from Paradise, and we know what *he* thinks about Eve's role in it. But what were Eve's feelings on the matter?

Ever since that first little incident in the garden, the recorded history of male-female relationships has had a decidedly male slant. However, this is not, as the quotations that follow illustrate, because women have had little to say.

WHAT WOMEN SAY ABOUT MEN

Women want mediocre men, and men
are working hard to be as
mediocre as possible.

MARGARET MEAD

If you want anything said, ask a man. If

you want anything done, ask

a woman.

MARGARET THATCHER

Behind every great man there is a
surprised woman.

MARYON PEARSON

■

If man is only a little lower than the
angels, the angels should reform.

MARY WILSON LITTLE

As long as you know most men are like children, you know everything.

COCO CHANEL

A man's home may seem to be his castle from the outside; inside, it is more often his nursery.

CLARE BOOTHE LUCE

I refuse to consign the whole male sex to the nursery. I insist on believing that some men are my equals.

BRIGID BROPHY

Probably the only place a man
can feel really secure is a maximum
security prison, except for the imminent
threat of release.

GERMAINE GREER

I like men to behave like men—
strong and childish.

FRANÇOISE SAGAN

I only like two kinds of men:
domestic and imported.

MAE WEST

One cannot be always laughing
at a man without now and then
stumbling on something witty.

JANE AUSTEN

If you talk about yourself, he'll think you're boring. If you talk about others, he'll think you're a gossip. If you talk about him, he'll think you're a brilliant conversationalist.

LINDA SUNSHINE

The average man is more interested
in a woman who is interested in him
than he is in a woman—any woman—
with beautiful legs.

MARLENE DIETRICH

Men are always ready to respect
anything that bores them.

MARILYN MONROE

■

The only place men want depth in
a woman is in her décolletage.

ZSA ZSA GABOR

Men are those creatures with two
legs and eight hands.

Jayne Mansfield

■

Men are beasts, and even beasts
don't behave as they do.

Brigitte Bardot

A gentleman is a patient wolf.

HENRIETT TIARKS

■

Give a man a free hand and he'll
run it all over you.

MAE WEST

Latins are tenderly enthusiastic.
In Brazil they throw flowers at you.
In Argentina, they throw themselves.

MARLENE DIETRICH

Whenever I date a guy, I think,
is this the man I want my children to
spend their weekends with?

RITA RUDNER

I like to wake up each morning feeling
a new man.

JEAN HARLOW

■

I feel like a million—but one at a time.

MAE WEST

Men make love more intensely at 20,

but make love better, however, at 30.

CATHERINE II OF RUSSIA

■

No nice men are good at getting taxis.

KATHARINE WHITEHORN

I never married because I have three
pets at home that answer the same
purpose as a husband. I have a dog that
growls every morning, a parrot that
swears all afternoon, and a cat that
comes home late at night.

MARIE CORELLI

I think every woman is entitled to a middle husband she can forget.

ADELA ROGERS ST. JOHN

It is ridiculous to think that you can spend your entire life with just one person. Three is about the right number. Yes, I imagine three husbands would do it.

CLARE BOOTHE LUCE

Marrying a man is like buying something you've been admiring for a long time in a shop window. You may love it when you get home, but it doesn't always go with everything else in the house.

JEAN KERR

Being a bachelor is the first requisite
of a man who wishes to form the perfect
household.

BEVERLY NICHOLS

The trouble with some women is that they get all excited about nothing—and then marry him.

CHER

A husband is what is left of the lover
after the nerve is extracted.

HELEN ROWLAND

A man in love is incomplete until he
is married. Then he's finished.

ZSA ZSA GABOR

If love means never having to say you're sorry, then marriage means always having to say everything twice. Husbands, due to an unknown quirk of the universe, never hear you the first time.

ESTELLE GETTY

Before marriage a man will lay awake
all night thinking about something you
said; after marriage, he'll fall asleep
before you finish saying it.

HELEN ROWLAND

An archaeologist is the best husband a
woman can have. The older she gets,
the more interested he is in her.

AGATHA CHRISTIE

There is so little difference between
husbands, you might as well keep
the first.

ADELA ROGERS ST. JOHN

Husbands are like fires. They go out if unattended.

ZSA ZSA GABOR

A man in the house is worth two
in the street.

MAE WEST

I have yet to hear a man ask for advice on how to combine marriage and a career.

GLORIA STEINEM

None of you (men) ask for anything—
except everything, but only so long as
you need it.

DORIS LESSING

In passing, also, I would just like to say
that the first time Adam had a chance
he laid the blame on women.

LADY NANCY ASTOR

Men and women, women and men.
It will never work.

ERICA JONG

A woman needs to know but one man well to understand all men; whereas, a man may know all women and not understand one of them.

HELEN ROWLAND

Getting along with men isn't what's truly important. The vital knowledge is how to get along with a man.
One man.

PHYLLIS McGINLEY

A good man doesn't just happen.
They have to be created by us women.
A guy is a lump, like a doughnut. So
first you gotta get rid of all the stuff
his mom did to him. And then you
gotta get rid of all that macho crap they
pick up from beer commercials. And
then there's my personal favorite,
the male ego.

ROSEANNE ARNOLD

The only time a woman really succeeds in changing a man is when he is a baby.

NATALIE WOOD

■

I married beneath me—all women do.

LADY NANCY ASTOR

Women are not men's equals in anything except responsibility. We are not their inferiors, either, or even their superiors. We are quite simply different races.

PHYLLIS McGINLEY

Men are too emotional to vote. Their
conduct at baseball games and political
conventions shows this, while their
innate tendency to appeal to force
renders them particularly unfit for the
task of government. . . . Man's place is
in the armory.

ALICE DUER MILLER

If the world were a logical place, men
would ride side-saddle.

RITA MAE BROWN

If a man watches three football games in a row, he should be declared legally dead.

ERMA BOMBECK

The more I see of men, the more
I like dogs.

MADAME DE STAËL

His mother should have thrown him
away and kept the stork.

MAE WEST

Giving a man space is like giving a dog a computer: Chances are he will not use it wisely.

BETTE-JANE RAPHAEL

The male is a domestic animal, which,
if treated with firmness and kindness,
can be trained to do most things.

JILLY COOPER

Man reaches the highest point of
lovableness at 12 to 17—to get it back,
in a second flowering, at the age of
70 to 90.

ISAK DINESEN

A woman who strives to be like a man
lacks ambition.

ANONYMOUS

Whatever women do they must do twice as well to be thought of as half as good. Luckily, this is not difficult.

CHARLOTTE WHITTON

Any woman can fool a man if she wants to and if he's in love with her.

AGATHA CHRISTIE

If it wasn't for women, men would still
be hanging from trees.

MARILYN PETERSON

Can you imagine a world without men? No crime and lots of happy, fat women.

MARION SMITH

Women speak because they wish to speak; whereas, a man speaks only when driven to speech by something outside himself—like, for instance, he can't find any clean socks.

JEAN KERR

One of the things being in politics has
taught me is that men are not a
reasoned or reasonable sex.

MARGARET THATCHER

Success has made failures of many
men.

CINDY ADAMS

■

Fortune does not change men. It
unmasks them.

SUZANNE NECKER

Beware of the man who praises women's liberation; he is about to quit his job.

ERICA JONG

Don't accept rides from strange men,

and remember all men are strange

as hell.

ROBIN MORGAN

Never refer to any part of his body
below the waist as "cute" or "little";
never expect him to do anything about
birth control; never ask if he changes
his sheets seasonally; never request that
he sleep in the wet spot.

C. E. CRIMMINS

Beware of men who cry. It's true that
men who cry are sensitive and in touch
with feelings, but the only feelings they
tend to be sensitive to and in touch with
are their own.

NORA EPHRON

Don't marry a man to reform him—
that's what reform schools are for.

MAE WEST

It is always incomprehensible to a man
that a woman should refuse an offer
of marriage.

JANE AUSTEN

Men, being conditioned badly, are always feeling nooses closing around their necks, even dumpy boors no girl would take on a bet.

CYNTHIA HEIMEL

A girl can wait for the right man to come along, but in the meantime that still doesn't mean she can't have fun with all the wrong ones.

CHER

A woman has got to love a bad man
once or twice in her life to be thankful
for a good one.

MARJORIE KINNAN RAWLINGS

If you never want to see a man again,
say, "I love you. I want to marry you.
I want to have children"—they leave
skid marks.

RITA RUDNER

It's not the men in my life that count,

it's the life in my men.

Mae West

I require only three things of a man.
He must be handsome, ruthless,
and stupid.

DOROTHY PARKER

There are only two kinds of men—the
dead and the deadly.

HELEN ROWLAND

■

Macho does not prove mucho.

ZSA ZSA GABOR

The text of this book was set in Electra,

and the initial caps were set in Parisian

by Dix Type Inc., Syracuse, New York.

Design by Diane Stevenson/Snap-Haus Graphics.

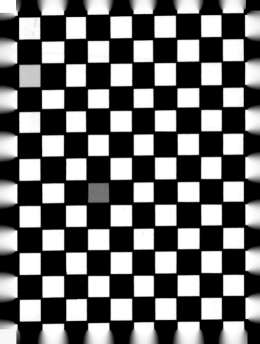